Human Impact
on the Environment

Elizabeth Rose

The Rosen Publishing Group's
PowerKids Press™
New York

For Flannery Emma and Emma Bean

Published in 2006 by The Rosen Publishing Group, Inc.
29 East 21st Street, New York, NY 10010

First Edition

Editor: Rachel O'Connor
Book Design: Albert Hanner

Photo Credits: Cover © Premium Stock/Corbis; p. 4 © Larry Lee Photography/Corbis; p. 5 © Premium Stock/Corbis; p. 7 © Image Works; p. 8. © Corbis; p. 9 (top) © Pete Saloutos/Corbis; p. 9 (bottom) Beth A. Keiser/AP Wide World Photography; p. 11 © Jon Feingersh/Corbis; p. 12 © George D. Lepp/Corbis; p. 13 (top) © Paul Barton/Corbis; p. 13 (bottom) Gunter Marx Photography/Corbis; p. 15 (top) © Craig Tuttle/Corbis; p. 15 (bottom) © Gallo Images/Corbis; pp. 16, 19 (bottom) © Royalty-Free/Corbis; p. 17 © Robert Landau/Corbis; p. 19 (top) Michael St. Maur Sheil/Corbis; p. 21 (top) © Ron Sanford/Corbis; p. 21 (middle) © Bettmann/Corbis; p. 21 (bottom) © Reuters/Corbis; p. 22 © Owaki Kulla/Corbis.

Library of Congress Cataloging-in-Publication Data

Rose, Elizabeth.
   Human impact on the environment / Elizabeth Rose.— 1st ed.
      p. cm. — (The life science library)
   Includes index.
   ISBN 1-4042-2822-5 (lib. bdg.)
   1. Human ecology—Juvenile literature. 2. Nature—Effect of human beings on—Juvenile literature. I. Title. II. Series: Life science library (New York, N.Y.)

   GF48.R33 2006
   304.2—dc22

                                        2004027049

Manufactured in the United States of America

Contents

The Environment Is All Around

People get coal, oil, and gas from the environment. Pictured here is an oil rig, which is used to drill for oil buried in rocks under water. Some oil rigs are built in water that is up to 1 mile (1.6 km) deep. Oil can be used to heat our houses and to help run our cars.

The **environment** is what we call our natural world. Everything around us, living and nonliving, is part of the environment. All living things get air, water, and sunshine from the environment. These are necessary for **survival**. The environment also provides dirt in which plants can grow. Plants feed both us and the animals we eat. People help the environment when we plant a garden or a tree, protect a forest, or clean up a lake. However, people also hurt the environment by throwing garbage into rivers and lakes, building factories that pollute the air, and forgetting to take care of our surroundings.

Your environment makes it possible for you to be alive. A clean environment is also full of beautiful things, such as lakes, flowers, trees, and mountains. These things are as important to a healthy environment as are clean water, fresh air, and sunshine.

Changing the Environment

Early people were not able to make a lot of changes to the environment. They did not know how to use tools, so they could not build cities, make roads, or even use fire to keep warm. They made use of the **resources** the environment offered but had little effect on their surroundings. Then people learned how to use tools and fire. They also learned how to farm the land and grow their own food. This meant that people could stay in one area instead of moving all the time to find food. Farming meant changing the environment. People began to clear forests, dam rivers, and keep animals such as cows and sheep for food. All these changes affected the environment.

This drawing shows an early family making use of the resources in their environment. They have made weapons to hunt animals and prepare them for food. They have cut wood from trees to make a fire to cook the animals, and to keep themselves warm. When early people found enough resources in one place, they were able to settle and make their home there. If the environment provided few resources, however, they would have to keep moving in search of food and shelter.

Urban Growth

The Industrial Revolution began in America around 1800. During this time electrical power was discovered and machines began to replace the work of people. Factories sprang up in the big cities, creating a lot of pollution that harmed the environment.

Did you know that New York City used to be **swamps**, forests, and meadows? Cities allow a lot of people to live in a small space, but they also greatly change the environment. One of the biggest ways that people change the environment is simply by growing in numbers. The human population today is nearly six and one-half billion. As the population grows, so do people's needs for more houses, roads, factories, and food. These changes can pollute the environment and can crowd out the plants and animals that share our environment. This crowding can lead to plants and animals becoming **endangered**, or even **extinct**.

Seattle, Washington, is shown here. Cities such as this use a lot of resources, such as electricity, coal, oil, and water. Just imagine how much electricity it takes to light up all the cities around the world!

The human population is always growing. However, Earth is not getting any bigger. One of humankind's biggest challenges is to figure out where people can live without destroying the habitat that plants and animals need to survive.

Gone Forever

When an animal becomes extinct, it is gone forever. This was the fate of the dodo, a flightless bird that once lived on the island of Mauritius, located in the Indian Ocean. Sailors who landed on the island in the 1600s hunted the dodo for meat and for sport. People also brought rats and dogs to the island. They ate the dodos' eggs. By 1681, the dodo was completely extinct, never to be seen again. Today animals and plants that are in danger of becoming extinct are usually protected by law. These animals and plants are known as endangered **species**. The main cause of extinction today is loss of **habitat**.

Giant pandas are facing extinction because people are taking over pandas' habitats. In November 2004, the total number of threatened or endangered plant and animal species in the United States alone was 1,264. Unless we learn to take better care of these animals and plants, scientists believe that thousands of animals may become extinct over the next 20 years.

Farming and the Environment

When farmers spray fertilizer on their crops, the chemicals can get into our bodies when we eat the plants that have been sprayed. The chemicals can also harm us when we eat animals that might have eaten the sprayed plants.

Cities are not the only things that change the environment. Farms can change it, too. In order to farm, farmers must cut down any forests on their land. They also often replace meadows and fields with crops such as hay or corn. This means that the animals that lived in the forests or the fields must find new homes.

Some farmers use poisonous **chemicals** to kill insects or to **fertilize** their farms. They can also harm the animals that eat insects, such as birds and bats. Today many farmers are growing their food without the use of these harmful chemicals. This kind of farming is called organic farming.

Organic farming does less harm to the environment because it does not poison the soil or the water in which plants are grown. Next time you are in a grocery store, look for food that is marked organic.

One of the reasons forests are cut down is to provide land for farming. However, the soil that is left after a forest has been cleared is usually not of good quality. As a result the land's use for agriculture usually lasts only a few short years.

13

The Disappearing Rain Forest

Clearing forests for farming and lumber can cause huge problems for the environment. This kind of clearing, called clear-cutting, is a particular problem in the **rain forest**. At least one-half of the world's species live in Earth's rain forests. There used to be more than 4 billion acres (1.6 billion ha) of rain forest on Earth. Today less than half of that amount remains. Clear-cutting the rain forest destroys the habitat for the plants and animals that need to live there. It can also cause floods. This is because trees soak up rain. When trees are cleared in huge numbers, the rain runs into rivers instead. This causes floods. Many animals and people have died in floods caused by clear-cutting.

Every year an area about the size of Wisconsin is being cleared from Earth's rain forest. The soil that is left behind after clearing a rain forest is not good soil. This is because the rich top layer has been washed away. This soil is good only for growing crops or feeding animals for a few years. After that it becomes useless.

The red-ruffed lemur lives in the rain forests of Madagascar. It is losing its habitat because of the logging of the rain forest to make farms. The red-ruffed lemur is listed as critically endangered, which means that it may be extinct very soon.

Air Pollution

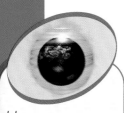

Here you can see Earth surrounded by the ozone layer. This is what protects us from the burning rays of the Sun. Without the ozone layer, there could be no life on Earth. Unfortunately, the ozone layer is being worn away by poisons that people release into the air.

The changes people make to the environment can cause different kinds of pollution. For example, air pollution is caused by cars, factories, dry-cleaning plants, power plants, air conditioners, and coal fires. It is a big problem all over the world. Smog is a kind of air pollution that takes the form of a yellowish haze in the air. Smog is made up of a gas called ozone.

Ozone is a gas that usually exists high up in our **atmosphere**. It protects us from the harmful rays of the Sun. However, ozone is harmful when it is near the ground.

Some cities, such as Los Angeles in California, have smog problems. These cities keep track of the amount of smog in their air every day. When the level of smog is high, city officials ask people to stay inside. Smog hurts peoples' and animals' lungs, making it hard for them to breathe. Smog can also cause headaches, chest pains, and coughing in people and animals when they breathe it in.

Water Pollution

The next time you see a piece of garbage on the street, or a candy wrapper floating in a stream, ask yourself where that garbage will end up. The answer is in the ocean. Anything that washes into streams will end up in the ocean. Some cities also dump their garbage and dirty water from toilets right in the ocean. All this dumping is very harmful for the ocean and for the animals and plants that live there. Another form of water pollution is called acid rain. Acid rain happens when chemicals and gases from factories and cars blow into the air. Then they **dissolve** in water vapor that is present in Earth's atmosphere. The gases and chemicals then fall as acid rain onto Earth, killing trees and plants.

When we dump our waste in rivers and oceans we are causing great harm to our environment and to ourselves. Water is necessary for everything on Earth to grow and survive. Increasingly the water we drink is becoming polluted, which can cause illnesses. In the poorer parts of the world, polluted water can even be the cause of many deaths.

Water covers around 70 percent of Earth's surface. The fish and other living things in this water can be harmed or killed by pollution. This waste can be in the form of oil that spills accidentally during drilling on an oil rig in the ocean.

Making Changes

As you can see, people can change the environment in unhealthy ways. The good news is there are groups of people around the world fighting to save the environment. The World Wildlife Fund, or WWF, is an organization that helps get laws passed to protect endangered animals and to preserve lands. Also, in California, farmers are beginning to use **predators** such as bats to eat insects instead of using chemicals. Most cities in America have recycling programs. This means that when you separate your glass, plastic, and paper garbage, they can be broken down and used again. There is a lot more work to do, but people are beginning to realize how important it is to protect our environment.

The California sea otter is one animal that the WWF has helped. People thought the California sea otter was extinct until a few were found in 1938. Because of careful work to protect them, there are now around 2,500 California sea otters.

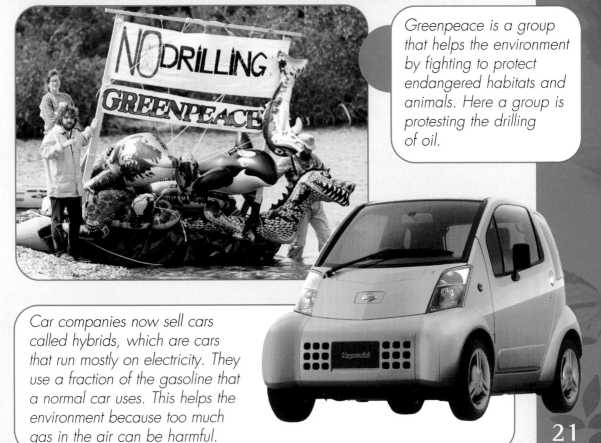

Greenpeace is a group that helps the environment by fighting to protect endangered habitats and animals. Here a group is protesting the drilling of oil.

Car companies now sell cars called hybrids, which are cars that run mostly on electricity. They use a fraction of the gasoline that a normal car uses. This helps the environment because too much gas in the air can be harmful.

What Can You Do?

The next time you are in a fast-food restaurant, try taking one paper napkin instead of a handful. Paper comes from trees, and the less paper you use, the more trees you are saving.

What can you do to help the environment? First of all you can speak out. Maybe you and your classmates could write a letter to your local representative about pollution in your area. You can also join a club that is fighting pollution, such as Kids Against Pollution. Recycling is another great way to help the environment. Even better than recycling is reducing, or cutting back on, what you use in the first place. For example, some adults now carry their own coffee cup instead of getting a paper cup at the coffee shop. Recycling and cutting down on waste are ways to help our environment stay safe, beautiful, and clean.

Glossary

atmosphere (AT-muh-sfeer) The layer of gases around an object in space. On Earth this layer is air.

chemicals (KEH-mih-kulz) Matter that can be mixed with other matter to cause changes.

dissolve (dih-SOLV) To break down.

endangered (en-DAYN-jerd) Describing an animal whose species or group has almost all died out.

environment (en-VY-ern-ment) All the living things and conditions of a place.

extinct (ek-STINKT) No longer existing.

fertilize (FUR-tuh-lyz) To encourage growth by adding something.

habitat (HA-bih-tat) The surroundings where an animal or a plant naturally lives.

predators (PREH-duh-terz) Animals that kill other animals for food.

rain forest (RAYN FOR-est) A thick forest that receives a large amount of rain during the year.

resources (REE-sors-ez) Supplies or sources of energy or useful items.

species (SPEE-sheez) A single kind of living thing. All people are one species.

survival (sur-VY-val) Staying alive.

swamps (SWOMPS) Wetlands with a lot of trees and bushes.

Index

A
acid rain, 18

C
chemicals, 12, 18, 20
cities, 8, 12, 18
clear-cutting, 14

D
dodo, 10

E
endangered species, 8, 10, 20
extinction, 8, 10

F
farms, 6, 12
floods, 14

H
habitat, loss of, 10, 14

O
organic farming, 12
ozone, 16

P
pollution, 4, 8, 16, 22
population growth, 8

predators, 20

R
rain forest, 14
recycling, 20

S
smog, 16

W
World Wildlife Fund (WWF), 20

Web Sites

Due to the changing nature of Internet links, PowerKids Press has developed an online list of Web sites related to the subject of this book. This site is updated regularly. Please use this link to access the list:

www.powerkidslinks.com/lsl/impactenv/